DRAMA CLASSIC.

The Drama Classics series aims to offer the world's greatest plays in affordable paperback editions for students, actors and theatregoers. The hallmarks of the series are accessible introductions, uncluttered texts and an overall theatrical perspective.

Given that readers may be encountering a particular play for the first time, the introduction seeks to fill in the theatrical/historical background and to outline the chief themes rather than concentrate on interpretational and textual analysis. Similarly the play-texts themselves are free of footnotes and other interpolations: instead there is an end-glossary of 'difficult' words and phrases.

The texts of the English-language plays in the series have been prepared taking full account of all existing scholarship. The foreign-language plays have been newly translated into a modern English that is both actable and accurate: many of the translators regularly have their work staged professionally.

Edited until his early death by Kenneth McLeish, the Drama Classics series continues with his aim of providing a first-class library of dramatic literature representing the best of world theatre.

Associate editors:
Professor Trevor R. Griffiths
Dr. Colin Counsell
School of Arts and Humanities
University of North London

DRAMA CLASSICS *the first hundred*

*The publishers welcome
suggestions for further titles*

DRAMA CLASSICS

LYSISTRATA

by

Aristophanes

translated by Patric Dickinson

edited and introduced by
Kenneth McLeish

NICK HERN BOOKS

London

www.nickhernbooks.co.uk

A Drama Classic

Lysistrata first published in Great Britain in this revised edition of Patric Dickinson's translation as a paperback original in 1996 by Nick Hern Books Limited, 14 Larden Road, London W3 7ST.

Patric Dickinson's translation originally published by Oxford University Press in 1957.

Typeset by Country Setting, Kingsdown, Kent CT14 8ES
Printed by Bookmarque, Croydon, Surrey

A CIP catalogue record for this book is available from the British Library

ISBN 1 85459 325 0

Introduction

Aristophanes (c. 450-380BC)

Aristophanes was the son of a wealthy man. He inherited property (perhaps a fruit-farm or nut-farm) on the island of Aegina in the Saronic Gulf near Athens. He wrote forty comedies for performance at the Theatre of Dionysos in Athens, and eleven of them still survive. Fifth-century Athens was small (some 300,000 inhabitants), and produced more than its share of people of world distinction: figures such as Alcibiades, Euripides, Pericles, Pheidias, Socrates and Thucydides. Aristophanes' surviving work, and admiring comments by his contemporaries, suggest that even in such company, he was one of the city's most dazzling lights. Despite attempts at censorship by thin-skinned individuals (for example, the war-leader Kleon), he regularly won prizes and was at the head of his profession for a quarter of a century.

Aristophanes was born in the period of glittering greatness which Athens enjoyed after the defeat of a vast Persian invasion-force in 480-479BC. During the 'Fifty Years', as the Athenians called it, the Parthenon was built on the Acropolis (to house a thirteen-metre-high statue of the goddess Athene, complete with war-spear, Gorgon shield and the golden helmet which features in the 'pregnancy' scene of *Lysistrata*), the arts flourished, and Athens' merchants and sailors made the city the hub of a large and prosperous empire. Then, in 431BC, just as Aristophanes himself reached his twenties, the Peloponnesian War broke out between Athens and Sparta, her former ally against the Persians, and Athenian prosperity began to wane.

Although the Peloponnesian War was fought between two independent states and their allies, it was Greek against Greek, as vicious as any civil war. It lasted for 27 years, the time of Aristophanes' greatest productivity, and gave him a serious theme which propelled his comedy to greatness. Most of his leading characters are honest, ordinary men or women, disgusted at the way corrupt officials are prolonging the war. Their despair leads them to take extreme steps to end it. Lysistrata's plan is typical: she persuades the women of Greece to start a sex-strike which will end only when their men make peace. Other characters in his plays include frauds, confidence-tricksters and perverts of every kind – the scum of society which, in wartime, floats to the surface – and each comedy shows the leading character routing them in a flurry of insult and slapstick.

Athens' surrender in 404 BC was followed, within a few months, by the deaths of two of the fellow playwrights Aristophanes most admired, Sophocles and Euripides. He himself was in his mid or late forties and seems to have retired from full-time theatre work. In the next twenty years he wrote only half a dozen plays; he seems to have spent his time managing his estate, enjoying the company of friends (including Plato, who made him a character in his dialogue *The Symposium*) and encouraging the playwriting-career of his son Araros (none of whose work survives).

This slowing-down may have been due to the fact that, with the war over, Aristophanes' greatest theme was gone. There were also fewer opportunities to put on plays: for decades after the war, few new plays of any kind were produced. Aristophanes may also have wanted to avoid stealing any of Araros' limelight. Illness – a crippling stroke – has also been suggested. The one thing certain is that diminished activity was not due to loss of creative energy. Aristophanes' last two surviving plays, *Women in Power* (*Ekklesiazousai*) and *Wealth*, though in a different style from his earlier work, are just as lively and inventive.

Lysistrata: **What Happens in the Play**

Some twenty years into the Peloponnesian War, in the besieged city of Athens, Lysistrata ('disbander of armies') forms a plan to end the fighting. The play begins at dawn, outside the gates of the fortified Acropolis. (This setting had extra force in the original production, because the Theatre of Dionysos itself lay directly at the foot of the Acropolis wall.) Lysistrata has called together all the women in Greece and is waiting impatiently to see them.

The women finally arrive – representatives of many states, including the Spartan Lampito – and Lysistrata tells them her plan. Since the war is getting nowhere under men's control, and Greece is being torn to pieces, the only solution is for women to take over public affairs and manage them as successfully as they run their homes. While one group of women occupies the Acropolis (so gaining control of the Athenian armoury and war-treasury), the others, by withholding sex, will persuade their men to make peace. The women agree reluctantly, and swear an oath (on a phallic wineskin) to resist their husbands.

The women seize the Acropolis, and a group of old men arrives to besiege it and win it back. They build a bonfire to smoke the women out; the women shower it, and them, with water from the battlements. An Athenian magistrate arrives in a fury, and he and Lysistrata argue about whether men or women are better equipped to run affairs of state. The magistrate becomes ever more dismissive and arrogant, and finally the women strip him, dress him in women's clothes and conduct a mock funeral.

After an interlude, in which the old men and old women of the Chorus taunt each other, Lysistrata faces her followers in despair. One by one, the women are weakening and trying to slip away to meet their husbands. We see several defectors – one hurrying home to 'spread her wool', another needing to 'strip her flax', a third pretending to be in labour. Lysistrata packs them back inside. After another choral interlude, Kinesias ('randy') arrives. He is the young husband of one of Lysistrata's principal supporters, Myrrhine ('myrtle-blossom' or, in slang, 'sexpot'), and he is eager to have sex with her. Myrrhine keeps him tantalised while she fetches a bed, a mattress, a pillow, scented oil and other items – and then asks him point-blank to agree to peace, running inside when he refuses.

A Spartan herald now brings news that the men of Sparta are desperate. He is followed by the Spartan ambassadors, bristling equally with the pomposity of their office and with frustration. They and the Athenian ambassadors try to come to terms, but nothing succeeds until Lysistrata takes over and arranges a treaty, using a beautiful woman (Reconciliation) as a map of Greece. The ambassadors of both states go inside to sign the treaty, while the Chorus sing ironically of the delights of peace. The ambassadors come back, drunk, and the play ends in a whirl of song and dance.

Lysistrata

Lysistrata was first produced in 411BC, when Aristophanes (then in his mid-thirties) was at the height of his career. By this time, the Peloponnesian War had continued for an entire generation and must have seemed as if it would never end. The Athenians had suffered invasion, plague, defeat on land and sea (most recently, in 413BC, the destruction of a glittering war-fleet sent to conquer Syracuse in Sicily). City politics were bedevilled not so much with corrupt leadership (as had been the case earlier in the war), as with a kind of exhausted impotence, as if everything had been tried and nothing had succeeded. In the play, Lysistrata points out that there was hardly a family in Athens which had not lost a father, son or husband.

These desperate circumstances may have given the play's original production particularly sombre overtones, an edge of hysteria similar to the atmosphere in Weimar-republic cabaret in 1920s Germany or more recent war-set comedies such as Joseph Heller's 1960s novel *Catch-22* and the 1970s-80s film and TV series *M*A*S*H*. In works like these, questions of morality and ethics – how we should live our lives – cease to involve huge, global issues and are focused instead on everyday obsessions, fads and feuds. The constant presence of death gives each second of survival devastating significance – and offers the satirical writer scope for lacerating irony.

If the atmosphere of *Lysistrata*'s first performance was anything similar, the central suggestion of the play, that men should hand over the affairs of state to women, must have had a political and social sharpness hard to recapture today. Not only that, but to the (male) audience, it may have seemed just as surreal as the trips to Heaven or privatised peace-treaties which figure in other Aristophanic plots. Women, in the Athenians' much-vaunted 'democracy', had few rights. They were chattels of their husbands, expected to keep them-selves to themselves at home, not to walk outdoors unchaperoned or unveiled, and to confine their interests to domestic matters. There was serious debate (among men) not so much about the scale and nature of female intelligence, as about whether women had any reasoning powers at all. At one level, *Lysistrata* is a farce about frustration. But its underlying ideas – that the impotence of war can be symbolised by sexual frustration, that resolution is possible and that women may be better able than men to bring this about – must have resonated with the original spectators in a way which brilliantly challenged their (and, later, our) ideas of what 'farce' ought to be. Aristophanes' older contemporary (and possibly friend), Euripides, explored similar issues in such plays as *Women of Troy*, *Electra* and *Alcestis*. But in all surviving Greek literature, he and Aristophanes are the only writers known to deal with such uncompromising and (for their time) 'bizarre' ideas, and they are remarkable both for what they say and for the way they expand and explode conventional dramatic forms to say it.

Aristophanic Comedy

Aristophanes' work is sometimes called 'Old' comedy, to distinguish his plays from the 'New' comedy of such later writers as Menander in Greece and Plautus and Terence in Rome. 'Old' comedy is surreal and fantastical, and its butts are specific individuals or current political ideas. 'New' comedy is realistic, and its satire is directed at human nature at large. 'New' comedy became the ancestor of most Western 'literary' comedy, of the character-based kind written by such authors as Shakespeare, Molière, Sheridan or Wilde. 'Old' comedy, with its slapstick routines, its physical energy and its music and dance, influenced other kinds of comedy, those once dismissed as 'low': circus, music-hall, variety, stand-up, film and TV slapstick – styles whose potential has only recently begun to be rediscovered by practitioners and scholars of what is loftily called 'legitimate' theatre.

Aristophanes developed his kind of comedy out of the earlier satyr-plays, performed with tragedies at festivals of Dionysos. On each festival day, three tragedies were followed by a satyr-play designed to provide a rumbustious contrast to the more serious items. The action was fast, funny, full of music and dance (notably from the chorus of Satyrs, complete with goats' legs, grotesque masks and enormous, artificial phalluses), and the plays were unblushingly obscene. There was always a happy ending: whereas tragedies showed heroes grappling with inexorable destiny, satyr-plays explored the fun of life.

It was Aristophanes' stroke of genius to develop this carefree, bawdy spectacle into a form of comedy which allowed him to make serious points in a light way, to explore the dilemmas of human life and the follies and failings of his contemporaries. In most of his surviving plays, the hero opens the action by complaining of some insoluble problem: unpayable debts in *Clouds*, the awfulness of Athenian life in *Birds*, the corruptness of politicians in *Knights*, the lack of good poets in *Frogs*, the endlessness of war in *Acharnians*, *Peace* and above all *Lysistrata*. The hero then announces that he or she has devised a way to solve this problem, and proceeds to put it into practice. The way chosen is always surreal – flying to Heaven to bring back the goddess of Peace (*Peace*), going to the Underworld to bring back a poet from the 'good old days' (*Frogs*), making a private peace-treaty with Sparta (*Acharnians*). But once the deed is done, it works, and the hero's fantasy-world becomes the play's reality.

Once fantasy is reality, anything is possible. Birds, clouds, corpses, dogs, gods, monsters, statues, even pots and pans turn into characters, and the hero talks on equal terms with them, as if it were the most natural thing in the world. As in dreams, not only is anything possible, but the unlikely is treated as if it is the most ordinary thing in the world. How do you fly to Heaven? You feed a dung-beetle until it's big enough to carry you. How do you become a bird? You chew the magic herb 'wing-wort' and grow wings. How do you force the gods to do what you want? You build a wall between Heaven and Earth, block their sacrifices and starve them into submission.

If surreal events and characters are treated in a 'real' way, exactly the opposite happens to people and ideas from the real world of the audience. Aristophanes regularly takes real people (Euripides, Socrates, politicians such as Kleon and Pericles, generals such as Lamachos, even the priest of Dionysos who sat enthroned at each stage performance and the prostitutes who worked down the road from the theatre) and brings them into the action, under their own names. He regularly mentions ideas currently in the (real) air of Athens: political theories, snippets of gossip, the kind of stories which would make the news in today's tabloids. He quotes from (real) Greek tragedy, poetry, oracles, hymns, proclamations and prayers, using the actual words. And whenever this happens, the people, stories and quotations fail absolutely to fit the fantasy reality which the hero's surreal deed has created. Euripides and Socrates are fools, the politicans and generals are rogues, the ideas and quotations are ridiculous.

Nowadays we are used to this in comedy, but not in comic plays. Stand-up comedians use the same techniques, and their acts depend on creating a surreal world in which anything at all is possible –

except that respect should be shown to people and events dragged in from real life. Also like stand-up comedians, Aristophanes' characters often break out of the created 'reality' of the show, to talk directly about the conditions of the performance they are giving: the weather, the audience, the meanness of the management, their own physical health, the strangeness of other performers – tiny obsessions of the moment, belonging to the actor rather than to the character in the story but still mentioned *by* that character.

In the midst of all such topical references, and among the jabs and jibes of satire, a modern comedian can still put across a sustained point of view about 'real' events in general – and the same is true of Aristophanes. In particular, a consistent attitude towards war and politics runs through all his plays and gives his work its bite. This view is that, unlike great conflicts of the past and despite grand and noble achievements, the Peloponnesian War is a disaster. It is destroying the greatness of Athens, is against the interests and wishes of ordinary people, and is kept going only because generals and politicians are too incompetent or corrupt to end it.

The fact that such ideas could be put across consistently for twenty years, in a city dominated by the war and ruled by the very politicians and generals Aristophanes mocks by name, shows not only courage on his part, but a remarkably tolerant state of mind in his audience and the city authorities. Perhaps the authorities regarded his plays as safety valves, allowing people to let off steam in a comparatively harmless way. Modern politicians tolerate even the most savage caricatures and cartoons of themselves – indeed, many collect them. There are many recorded instances of comic writers changing the way we look at the world, but very few of them affecting the way things are actually run.

At first hearing, it may sound as if 'Old' comedy is complex and multi-faceted, too 'packed' nowadays for easy understanding or enjoyment. The mixture is certainly rich. But Aristophanes is anything but difficult. His plots are clear, his jokes and routines are of inspired lunacy, and his characters are universally recognisable. His heroes are grown-up children, and what they say and do – in short, his comedy – is neither shameless nor vulgar (as is sometimes claimed) but blessed with glorious, life-enhancing innocence.

Original Staging

Lysistrata was written for the Lenaia festival of 411BC. The Lenaia was held each year in honour of Dionysos, in the god's shrine and theatre at the foot of the Acropolis. The festival's name is associated with *lenos* ('wine-vat') or *lenai* ('maenads' – Dionysos' ecstatic worshippers), or possibly with both, and scholars think that the festival was held to celebrate the ceremonial first opening, in January or early February, of wine made the previous year. At this time of year, the weather was too rough for sea-travel, so there were few visitors in Athens (as compared with the larger dramatic festival, the Great Dionysia, held later in the year). The events of the Lenaia, therefore, had a domestic, 'family' tone, allowing frankness and concentration on local issues – something Aristophanes himself claims in the opening speech of *Acharnians*, written for the Lenaia of 425BC.

Although some tragedies were performed at the Lenaia, the main focus of the festival was comedy. On each festival day, a different comedy was performed, in competition with the others. Aristophanes was one of some half-dozen regular comic writers, and there were also occasional entries by 'one-work' playwrights. Performances took place in the Theatre of Dionysos – not the surviving stone theatre (which dates from the following century) but its humbler and slightly smaller predecessor. The focus of the action was a large circle (the *orchestra* or 'dancing place'), and the audience sat in horseshoe-shaped, tiered rows on the slope leading up to the Acropolis walls, looking down towards the shrine of Dionysos, whose wall formed a backdrop to the acting-area. This acting-area included a long, rectangular stage, slightly raised from the level of the *orchestra*; on it there were either buildings painted on scenery, or (some say) real buildings, to provide a setting for the action.

Although little survives of the ancient theatre, scholars agree that it was vast. The audience may have numbered as many as 14,000 people, all male. The *orchestra* was some 22 metres in diameter, and the acting-area was 22 metres long by 8 metres deep. All performances took place in the open air, in natural light. Though references to times of day are common in the plays, these references themselves were enough to 'set' the time of the action, and no attempt was made to simulate the dawn, evening or blaze of noon which they described. The actors (3-5) and Chorus (24) were all male. The Chorus-members were amateurs, one chosen from each district of the city, as a way of honouring Dionysos at his own dramatic festival. The actors were all professionals. Some specialised in playing female roles, others (to judge by internal evidence in the texts) were dialect comedians, dancers or experts in comic song or slapstick. The pretty women who appear in several plays (for example Reconciliation in *Lysistrata*) may have been the only real females in the theatre: you could hire a slave for the day for less than the price of dinner.

In most surviving Greek plays, it hardly matters that the performers and the audience-members were all male, but in *Lysistrata* it may have been crucial to the effect. The text offers a gallery of different kinds of 'travesty' parts, in which men play femininity of all kinds: straight-forward (Lysistrata herself), seductive (Myrrhine), caricature crone (the old women of the 'female' Chorus). The play's arguments about putting the affairs of state in women's hands must have had extra pungency because they were spoken by men in drag to an audience of men. Comedy audiences were used to bizarre characters – wasps, centaurs, birds and so on – and in such an atmosphere, women who took political action may well have seemed equally fanciful. Aristophanes' text takes maximum advantage of such a reaction, both ironically and satirically: his female characters talk sense and his male characters are buffoons.

The playing of female parts by men, and the doubling and trebling of characters, was eased by the fact that all the actors wore character-masks. They divided the parts between them according to experience and rank in the company. The first actor played Lysistrata, the second actor two or three of the other main parts (perhaps doubling Lampito and the Spartan Ambassador), the third actor most of the other parts, and so on. In some Aristophanes plays, the leading role is outrage-ously farcical, with opportunities we would now associate with a leading comic actor or star comedian. Other plays, including *Lysistrata*, surround a 'serious' central character with grotesques and comedians of every kind. The Chorus sang and danced, its choreography and music arranged (by the author) to follow the (often complex) rhythms of the words. Unfortunately, the Greeks had no ways of notating music or dance-steps, with the result that none survive. Our only evidence for the music is the rhythm of the words; evidence for dance has to be gleaned from general descriptions in the text (for example,

'Look how they whirl and kick their heels') or from pictures on ornamental vases. Apart from that, there is no firm evidence about the look of the play. In some plays (*Birds* or *Clouds*, for example), costumes and choreography may have been spectacular. In others, including *Lysistrata*, 'ordinary' costumes may have been more appropriate, and the action seems to require less showy dance. (In *Lysistrata* the most spectacular dancing may have been saved for the last scene of all, when the Spartans and Athenians celebrate their peace.)

Editor's Note

Sadly, Patric Dickinson died before this edition could be prepared. Except for the spelling of some Greek words, and changes to a few slang expressions which have dated since the 1950s, the translation is as he left it. In the text, changes are marked with square brackets. Where the original translation used very long lines, too many words to fit across our pages, I have divided them in two. Apart from that, my contributions are this introduction and the glossary and pronunciation guide on page 75. It was radio productions of Patric's translations in the 1950s which brought Aristophanes back to popularity in Britain after a long dark age, and it is a pleasure to acknowledge his contribution here. This edition, and those of his other Aristophanes versions which we shall reprint in due course, are affectionately dedicated to his memory.

Kenneth McLeish, 1996

Further Reading

K.J. Dover, *Aristophanic Comedy* (1972) is a useful introduction, good on the political background and the content and themes of each play. Kenneth McLeish, *The Theatre of Aristophanes* (1980) discusses the conditions in which Aristophanes worked, his style, and the way the plays may have been performed in the original theatre. C. H. Whitman, *Aristophanes and the Comic Hero* (1964) is a scholarly book about the way Aristophanes' themes are embodied in his leading characters – intellectually uncompromising material made accessible by Whitman's lucid style and his zest for Aristophanes and his work. Jeffrey Henderson, *The Maculate Muse* (1975) is a survey of every bawdy word and reference in Aristophanes: mind-boggling to read but essential to full understanding. Mary Renault, *The Mask of Apollo* (1966) is a historical novel set in the ancient Greek theatre, with a marvellously believable actor-hero.

Aristophanes: Key Dates

(NB *all dates are* BC)

525-456	Aeschylus
496-406	Sophocles
484-406	Euripides
c465	Theatre of Dionysos inaugurated
c450	Aristophanes born
431	Peloponnesian War begins
c428	Aristophanes' first play produced
425	*Acharnians* (Aristophanes' first surviving play)
424	*Knights*
423	*Clouds*
422	*Wasps*
421	*Peace*
415-413	Disastrous Athenian expedition to Sicily
414	*Birds*
411	*Lysistrata*; *Thesmophoriazousai*
405	*Frogs*
404	Surrender of Athens
c392	*Ekklesiazousai*
388	*Wealth*
c380	Aristophanes dies

LYSISTRATA

Characters

LYSISTRATA
KALONIKE
MYRRHINE
LAMPITO
MAGISTRATE
ATTENDANTS
STRATYLLIS
WOMEN (*of the force in the Acropolis*)
KINESIAS (*Myrrhine's husband*)
THEIR BABY
SLAVE
SPARTAN HERALD
SPARTAN AMBASSADORS
ATHENIAN AMBASSADORS
RECONCILIATION
ATHENIAN YOUTHS
PORTER
ATHENIAN BANQUET GUESTS
MUSICIANS
CHORUS (*of old men*)
CHORUS (*of women*)

Notes

In this version, the Spartans speak with a Lancashire accent.

A guide to pronunciation of the names is included in the Glossary, pages 75-80.

Athens. The scene is the slope from the Lower to the Upper City. In the background is the gateway to the Acropolis. It is daybreak. LYSISTRATA *is pacing up and down. She is in a flurry of impatience, and finally bursts out:*

LYSISTRATA
If they'd been asked to attend some Bacchic beano,
Some party for Pan, or Kolias, or Aphrodite,
You couldn't get through for the crush of revellers;
But now, there isn't a woman in sight, not a single
One . . . Well, here's my neighbour coming . . .

Enter KALONIKE.

Good morning, Kalonike.

KALONIKE
'Morning, Lysistrata. My dear, whatever's
The matter? You look fed up to the teeth. Stop frowning!
It doesn't suit you.

LYSISTRATA
Kalonike, I'm furious, and
It's the women, yes *women*. We're not to be relied on –
Don't all the men *love* to say so, and . . .

KALONIKE
But aren't we?

LYSISTRATA
I *told* them all to be here; I *said* it was most important,
And they've none of them come. They're simply hogging in bed.

KALONIKE

They'll come. You know, it's hard for a woman to get away:
You're pottering round your husband; you're chivvying a slave,
You're putting a baby to bed, or washing and feeding the brat . . .

LYSISTRATA

But there *are* other things, like *this*, *far* more important.

KALONIKE

But Lysistrata, *what*? Why've you called us? What's up?

LYSISTRATA

Something big.

KALONIKE

Is it really pressing?

LYSISTRATA

Biggest ever.

KALONIKE

Then why on earth isn't everybody here?

LYSISTRATA

Oh it's not that – they'd come quick enough for *that*.
No; it's an *idea*. Something I've *thought* of in bed,
Alone, awake in the night, tossing and turning.

KALONIKE

It must be a teaser to keep *you* tossing and turning.

LYSISTRATA

It is. So simple, so all-embracing. Just that the whole salvation
Of Greece depends on us women.

KALONIKE

On US? Then civilisation hangs by a thread!

LYSISTRATA

It depends on us, truly it does,
Whether the Peloponnesians are all annihilated –

KALONIKE

Let 'em be, I say, far better if they were!

LYSISTRATA

And all the Boeotians –

KALONIKE

All? Oh, please not the eels;
Surely you'd spare the *eels*?

LYSISTRATA

And as for the Athenians –
I can't bring myself to say it – you must supply my meaning.
But *if* all the women *did* come from Boeotia, the Peloponnese,
And all of us here came, too: we could save the entire country.

KALONIKE

But women? *Us* women? Sitting as pretty as flowers
In our saffron silks, and all made up, and moulded
In the long folds of our gowns and our feet in dainty shoes?
What wonders could *we* perform? What could we *do*?

LYSISTRATA

Just that. Those are the weapons I'm counting on to save us:
These saffron silks and dainty shoes and scent and make-up
And diaphanous nothings.

KALONIKE

Save us? *I'd* have . . . What d'you mean?

LYSISTRATA (*slowly and seriously*)

That men shall never take spears against each
other again . . .

KALONIKE

I'll put on my best dress . . .

LYSISTRATA

Never draw swords . . .

KALONIKE

I'll buy a new pair of shoes.

LYSISTRATA

Then wasn't it essential
For the women to come here?

KALONIKE

Walking's far too slow;
They ought to have flown.

LYSISTRATA

That's the Athenians all over:
Do everything too late – but I'm sorry not one
Woman's sailed up from the coast or over from Salamis.

KALONIKE

They were all manned by daybreak, too, I haven't a doubt.

LYSISTRATA

And the ones I absolutely counted on coming first,
The girls from Acharnai – there's not a sign of them.

KALONIKE

Theagenes' wife has consulted the oracle:
I'm afraid *she's* bound to come . . . But look, here *are* some women,
They're simply piling in.

Enter MYRRHINE *with a group of* WOMEN.

Hello!

(*To* LYSISTRATA)

Where've *they* sprung from?

LYSISTRATA

Anagyros.

KALONIKE

That means we've stirred up trouble.

MYRRHINE

Are we too late, Lysistrata? . . . Well . . . say *something*!

LYSISTRATA

I can't say much for you, Myrrhine, meandering up
So late for such an occasion.

MYRRHINE

I just couldn't find
My belt in the dark – but if this is really so urgent,
Tell us what it's about.

LYSISTRATA

No, we'll wait for a bit.
Till the Boeotians appear – and the Peloponnesians.

MYRRHINE

Yes, that's a good idea. Here's Lampito anyhow.

Enter LAMPITO *with a group of Spartan* WOMEN.

LYSISTRATA

Lampito, my sweet! Delighted to see you, darling,
How pretty you look! How healthy you Spartans are!
And my, what biceps! I believe you could throttle a bull.

LAMPITO

Eh, and I could that, and no mistake.
It's the gym I do, see? Just watch me do the fling,
And bat my bum with my heels!

LYSISTRATA

What magnificent breasts!

LAMPITO
Prod me like that,
And I feel like the fatted calf!

LYSISTRATA
Where does *this* girl come from?

LAMPITO
Boeotia and she's classy!

LYSISTRATA
Sweet Boeotian countryside,
The very plain of the Cyprian . . .

KALONIKE
And perfectly cropped and weeded.

LYSISTRATA
And this?

LAMPITO
She's a good girl. She's from Corinth.

LYSISTRATA
A good girl *and* from Corinth? Well, as far as I can *see* . . .

LAMPITO
Now tell me, who called up this gabble of girls?

LYSISTRATA
I did.

LAMPITO
Eh, did you now? And what's it all in aid of?

MYRRHINE
Yes, Lysistrata, tell us about this 'urgent business'.
What is it?

LYSISTRATA

Of course I'll tell you. But first, have you any objection
If I ask you one tiny question – all of you?

MYRRHINE

Ask whatever you like.

LYSISTRATA

Then – don't you all crave for the fathers
Of your children, away on service? – For I'm certain you've all
    got husbands
Away at the front.

KALONIKE

Five months in Thrace, worst luck,
Keeping watch on Eucrates.

MYRRHINE

Mine's seven months on Pylos.

LAMPITO

Mine's hardly in at the door, but he totes his equipment
And off again . . .

LYSISTRATA

Not even the ghost of a lover's
Been left us women. So – if I find a method of stopping the war,
Would you like it? Would you be with me?

MYRRHINE

You bet! Even if I have to pawn my mantle
And blow the proceeds on . . . well, on a party . . .

KALONIKE

I'd cut myself in half just like a flatfish,
And give away half for peace . . .

LAMPITO

I'd crawl to the top
Of Taügetos, to see peace again, I would.

LYSISTRATA

All right! I'll speak then. I'll let out my great secret!
Women! If we want to compel the men
To make peace, we must . . . it's imperative . . .

KALONIKE

Well, go on.

LYSISTRATA

Will you do it?

KALONIKE

Die if we don't!

LYSISTRATA

Then – NO SLEEPING WITH THEM. Total abstinence.
Why do you turn away? Where are you going?
Why do you bite your lips and shake your heads,
Turn pale and start to snivel? Will you do it,
Or won't you? Well?

MYRRHINE

Not me. I'll never do it.
Let the war go on!

KALONIKE

Nor me. Let the war go on!

LYSISTRATA

You – and you swore you'd cut yourself in half . . .

KALONIKE

Anything else you like – I'd go through fire
If you said I had to – but, Lysistrata, not that.
You must see, darling, not *that*: there's nothing like it.

LYSISTRATA

And you, Myrrhine?

MYRRHINE

Fire for me, too. Sorry.

LYSISTRATA

Women – what a miserable lot
We are! It's not surprising tragedies
Are written about us, nothing but beds and cradles,
Always the same old story, men and babies.
But Lampito – you're Spartan – if only *you'd*
Be on my side we might still pull it off:
Will you vote for me?

LAMPITO

Eh, but it's tough for women,
Sleeping alone all night, waiting for the cocks to crow.
Still if we must, we must. It's peace at any price.

LYSISTRATA

You darling, you're the only one!

KALONIKE

But if we *did*
Do . . . what you say (and I hope to heaven we won't
Have to) could you really *guarantee* peace that way?

LYSISTRATA

I'm certain of it.
Look here. We sit indoors, all tarted up,
In our most transparent things and obviously sexy,
We get the men worked up, bee-lined for bed,
And then when it comes to the point – walk out on them.
They'll make a treaty at once – you know they will.

LAMPITO

(Like Menelaus, coming to do her in,
Saw Helen's breasts and chucked his sword away.)

KALONIKE

But supposing they simply leave us?

LYSISTRATA

We must make
The best of the next best, as the proverb says.

KALONIKE

Proverbs aren't lovers. But suppose they grab us
And drag us to bed by force?

LYSISTRATA

Hang on to the door.

KALONIKE

Suppose they knock us about?

LYSISTRATA

Give in and sulk.
There's not much fun in raping your wife. If you need to,
Get at them in other ways. They'll soon give it up.
It's a poor look-out for a man if the woman won't play.

KALONIKE

Well, if you *really* think it'll work, I suppose
We'd better think so too . . .

LAMPITO

Now, Spartan husbands, we can jockey them
Into making peace without cheating. But how about
Your fickle Athenian bed-bugs – how'll you get any sense
Out of them?

LYSISTRATA

We'll fix *them* all right,
You needn't worry.

LAMPITO

Not worry? While they've got
Their triremes ready for sea; their treasury bulging with brass?

LYSISTRATA

But we've provided for that. We're proposing to occupy
The Acropolis this morning. It's a job for the *older* girls.
While *we* sit here at this . . . sexplanation, *they*,
Pretending to sacrifice, are seizing the Treasury now.

LAMPITO

Got everything sorted, you have – it might just work!

LYSISTRATA

Then come on, Lampito, let's make an oath
As quick as we can; then nothing can go wrong.

LAMPITO

Just say the words, love, I'll repeat the dose.

LYSISTRATA

Splendid! Who'll act as server? Don't stand there staring!
Set a shield hollow side up and fetch the sacrifice!

KALONIKE

Lysistrata, what *sort* of oath are we going to swear?

LYSISTRATA

Well, in the *Seven Against Thebes* they sacrificed a sheep.
Over a shield, I thought . . .

KALONIKE

But Lysistrata, *dear*,
One would *never* swear about *peace*, over a *shield* . . .

LYSISTRATA

What *shall* we do then?

KALONIKE

A white horse, would that do?

LYSISTRATA

A *white horse*, really, where could we get it from?

KALONIKE

What *shall* we swear on, then?

LYSISTRATA

I know. I tell you what *I'd* like.
Get me a big black bowl and put it hollow side up, and –
We'll sacrifice a skinful, no a jar full of Thasian WINE, and,
Swear not to add a drop of – WATER. How about that?

LAMPITO

That's a right good oath, I swear – there's more *in* that than
words.

LYSISTRATA

Then bring me the bowl and the wine-jar.

The jar is fetched. It's phallic-shaped.

KALONIKE

My dears, just look
What a beautiful jar! You couldn't help being delighted
With emptying that.

LYSISTRATA

Put down the bowl. Take hold of the victim.

She prays.

O goddess Persuasion, O loving cup,
Accept our offering, look with favour
Upon us women now and for ever . . .

KALONIKE (*intoning*)

'The fine red blood how bountifully it flows . . . '

LAMPITO (*parody*)

And, by Castor, how beautiful to my nose . . .

MYRRHINE (*dreamy*)

Let *me* be the first to take the oath, my dears . . .

KALONIKE *(sharply)*
By the goddess, NOT unless you draw first lot!

LYSISTRATA *(in command)*
Now, Lampito, all of you!
Put your hands on the cup,
Kalonike, you be spokeswoman:
Repeat whatever I say,
After me, word for word.
The rest of you confirm
And abide by it faithfully.

I will have no man come to me, neither lover nor husband.

KALONIKE
I will have no man come to me, neither lover nor husband.

LYSISTRATA
Though he comes like a battering ram . . . Speak!

KALONIKE
Though he comes like a battering ram . . . Oh god,
I'm weak at the knees, Lysistrata.

LYSISTRATA
I will live at home a virgin pure

KALONIKE
I will live at home a virgin pure

LYSISTRATA
In my flimsiest silk and enticingly made up

KALONIKE
In my flimsiest silk and enticingly made up

LYSISTRATA
So that my husband may particularly want me

KALONIKE
So that my husband may particularly want me

LYSISTRATA
But never willingly will I give myself to anyone

KALONIKE
But never willingly will I give myself to anyone

LYSISTRATA
And if he forces me

KALONIKE
And if he forces me

LYSISTRATA
I will be frigid and not respond to him.

KALONIKE
I will be frigid and not respond to him.

LYSISTRATA
I will not lift my legs to the ceiling

KALONIKE
I will not lift my legs to the ceiling

LYSISTRATA
Nor crouch like the lioness carved on the knife handle

KALONIKE
Nor crouch like the lioness carved on the knife handle

LYSISTRATA
Having sworn this oath may I drink from here

KALONIKE
Having sworn this oath may I drink from here

LYSISTRATA
But if I break it let my cup be filled with water.

KALONIKE
But if I break it let my cup be filled with water.

LYSISTRATA
Do you all swear this?

MYRRHINE
Oh yes, we *all* swear this.

LYSISTRATA
Then I'll finish the victim off!

KALONIKE
Steady, dear, fair shares! Let's show we're all friends here.

Female cheers and shouts, off.

LAMPITO
Eh, what's that hullabaloo?

LYSISTRATA
What I was telling you – the older women
Have occupied the Acropolis! Now, Lampito,
Get back to Sparta and organise things there
(But leave your friends as hostages). We'll reinforce
The others in the Acropolis and see
The doors are bolted fast.

KALONIKE
Won't the men come
And attack us soon?

LYSISTRATA
I couldn't care less about the men.
They can use what threats they like, they can use *fire*,
Those doors will not be opened unless we say so,
And only on our conditions . . .

KALONIKE

They won't, by Aphrodite!
If they're going to call us women insuperable and fiendish
Let's earn the reputation!

LAMPITO *leaves for Sparta. The rest disappear through the gates into the Acropolis. Then the* CHORUS OF OLD MEN *enters staggering under the weight of great bundles of faggots and lighted charcoal braziers.*

CHORUS OF MEN

Keep on, Drakes, easy does it, though you rub your shoulder
Raw with that great olive trunk. The older I get the less I
Know what's coming next, but I confess I never thought I'd
Be faced with such a shocking thing – did *you*, Strymodoros?
That these blighted sluts
We keep and feed, worse luck,
Should maul Athene's image,
Control the Acropolis
And stop us getting in
By bolting up the gates –
We must press on to the citadel, and be quick about it,
And stack it thick with faggots, and, Philourgos,
When we've ringed this persistent lot of plotters,
We'll fire the wood with our own hands and burn the whole
     boiling
(But first, that poisonous woman – Lykon's little darling),
Agreed?
Why, that Kleomenes, the first man to seize it,
Did *he* get away scot-free?
No! He surrendered to me,
For all his Spartan spirit,
Wearing only a rag of filthy cloth,
Unshaven, lousy, stinking,
Six years without a bath!
We besieged that fellah without a break, keeping watch at
     the gate,
Seventeen ranks of us sleeping at our posts . . .
And as for these pests
Whom even the gods hate (and so does Euripides)

Shall I do nothing in face of such flagrant defiance?
If I do, let my Marathon medals be torn from my breast!
But as for us all
The rest of the road
Is a one-in-four: we strive for the citadel
And how shall we haul
This without a moke?

How sharp on my shoulders lumps this load!
But it's got to be done
And the fire kept going,
It mustn't go out before we arrive:
So keep blowing, blowing –
Fffffff! The smoke!

O Herakles, it's dire!
What sparks flew up,
They bit at my brow – like a dog with rabies!
Must be Lemnos-fire –
And *that's* not a joke –
Or it couldn't have given me such a snap!
But, on to the top
Or Athene will suffer,
And when did she need help more than now,
Laches? Keep puffing, puffing –
Fffffff! The smoke!

Burning quite clear, thank heaven!
So let's unload our logs here,
Kindle a torch of vinewood,
And burst at the door like a battering-
Ram. And *then*, if the women
Don't open up when we ask 'em,
Set fire to the door and smother
The lot! Unload! Confound this
Smoke! Will no Samian general
Lend a hand? (My back's stopped aching.)
Up, coal! That's *your* job, brazier –
Fire the torch, I'll be first to brandish it!

Now, Victory, vaunt our trophy
Over these brazen bitches!

The CHORUS OF WOMEN *enter from the other side. For the
present the two choruses do not see each other.*

CHORUS OF WOMEN

I don't like the look of this. Am I too late to help them?
For I could hardly get at the spring to fill my bucket
What with the dark and the crowd, the confusion and clashing
    of pitchers,
The elbowing slaves, the jostling
Runaways; in the end
I jumped the queue and snatched this
Water I bring to succour
My burning comrades.

For I've heard those old devils saying
They're bringing heavy enough
Logs for a bath-furnace,
And they're making revolting threats
Against us women.
We're abominable, they say, they're going to burn us to ashes.
(O goddess, never, never may I see it, but see us instead
Saviours of Greece and its people from war and madness.)

(*Praying*)

Wherefore, O Golden-Helmet,
Protector, we hold thy temple;
And I entreat thine aid, Athene,
If any set fire to us down there
To bear water for us.
Wait a minute! What's this?

The CHORUSES *meet face to face. To* CHORUS OF OLD
MEN.

You men must be monsters –
You couldn't be anything else by the look of things.

CHORUS OF MEN

What a *remarkable* sight! Did you ever expect to see this?
A swarm of women standing guard in the gateway!

CHORUS OF WOMEN

What an insult! Take *us* for a swarm!
Let me tell you you haven't seen a thousandth of our forces!

CHORUS OF MEN

Phaidrias, shall we pluck these old mocking-birds,
And take a stick to their backs?

CHORUS OF WOMEN

Put down our pitchers, and then if they start something,
We won't be cluttered up.

CHORUS OF MEN

By god, a couple of slaps like Bupalos got
And they'll shut their traps.

CHORUS OF WOMEN

Get on then. Here I am. And I'm staying put.
Nobody else is going to have the pleasure . . .

STRATYLLIS

Of kicking you in the crutch!

CHORUS OF MEN

Shut up or I'll knock your old block off.

CHORUS OF WOMEN

Just try it! You dare lay a finger
On Stratyllis . . .

CHORUS OF MEN

Suppose I give her
A straight left – what'll you do?

CHORUS OF WOMEN
There won't be much *left* of you.
I'll tie your lungs in a love-knot, I'll tug out your guts . . .

CHORUS OF MEN (*mocking*)
Good old Euripides, you were right about women!
There isn't a sweeter creature . . .

CHORUS OF WOMEN
Rhodippe, up with the jug.

CHORUS OF MEN
What's the water *for*, you god-hated women?

CHORUS OF WOMEN
What's the fire *for*, you old foot-in-the-grave?

CHORUS OF MEN
You'll see who's for the pyre.

CHORUS OF WOMEN
You'll see what the water's for!

CHORUS OF MEN
You couldn't put out a fire-fly.

CHORUS OF WOMEN
Couldn't I? Well, we'll see!

CHORUS OF MEN
Why I don't roast you, I can't imagine.

CHORUS OF WOMEN
Got any soap? I'll give you a bath!

CHORUS OF MEN
A bath for me, you old bitch?

CHORUS OF WOMEN
Yes, a bath for a bridegroom!

Cackles of derisive laughter.

CHORUS OF MEN
What insolence – did you hear it?

CHORUS OF WOMEN
I can say what I like – I'm free.

CHORUS OF MEN
I'll stop your gab!

CHORUS OF WOMEN
I'll take care
You don't sit on the Bench again!

CHORUS OF MEN
Fire, set fire to her hair!

CHORUS OF WOMEN
Water, to your work, water!

They souse the OLD MEN *from their pitchers. The* OLD MEN
splutter and cough.

Was it *hot* enough?

CHORUS OF MEN
Stop it! Stop it!
What are you doing?

CHORUS OF WOMEN
Watering you!
To make you *bloom* again –

CHORUS OF MEN
But I'm withering, shivering, shrinking . . .

CHORUS OF WOMEN
You've got your fire to warm you . . .

Enter MAGISTRATE *with his four* ATTENDANTS.

MAGISTRATE
What, *another* outbreak of riot among the women?
Oh, these little drummings and continual orgies!
These Adonis laments from the roof-tops!
Why, I even heard one, sitting in the Assembly:
Demostratos – damn him – was proposing a motion
To sail to Sicily, or some such tomfoolery,
And there was his wife wailing 'Lament for Adonis'
And *he* roaring 'We must raise a force for Zakynthos'
And *she* yelling, half-tipsy on the roof-top,
'Weep for Adonis' and still the bellowing old blusterer
Boring on through it all – that's a typical example
Of this uncontrollable behaviour of women!

CHORUS OF MEN
And suppose you'd heard of their insufferable
Effrontery today? They abused us and soused us;
It makes us look as if we'd pissed in our tunics.

MAGISTRATE
And serve us right, by the sea-god! We're just as blameworthy
As *they* are. It was *we* taught them this attitude;
We sowed the wind, we must reap the whirlwind.
Just *look* at the way we men go on, in a shop:
'Oh goldsmith, remember the necklace
You made my wife – she was out dancing
Last night, and the clasp came off and I've got to
Run over to Salamis. If you've a *moment*,
Could you come round tonight, and fix her
A new clasp.' Well, I *ask* you. And another
Idiot goes to the cobbler, a randy bit of manhood,
With a kit a boy couldn't handle, and says,
'My wife's toe is so tender;
It's chafed by her sandal.

Could you come round about midday and fit her
A little bit looser?'
That's what things have come to!
And now here am I, a government official,
Come to get money out of the Treasury
To pay for oars, and the gates are barricaded
Right in my face by these rampant women!
I must put a stop to this nonsense.
Fetch me crowbars! Why are you goggling
There, you slacker? Snooping about for an inn?
Crowbars! Shove these crowbars under the gates:
You, over *there*! I'll take this. Now. One – two – three –

But the gates open and there stands LYSISTRATA.

LYSISTRATA
You needn't force the gates. I'm coming out
Of my own accord – and it isn't crowbars you want,
It's common sense.

MAGISTRATE
Really? You . . . you – where's my officer?
Arrest her! Tie her hands behind her back.

LYSISTRATA
By Artemis! The tip of a finger on me,
And public servant or not, his private service
'll be over!

MAGISTRATE (*to his men*)
Are you afraid? You there, go with him,
Tackle her round the waist, tie her up, get on with it!

Enter KALONIKE.

KALONIKE
By Hekate! A finger on *her* and I'll spread
Your guts on the road!

MAGISTRATE

My guts on the road, eh?
Officer! Handcuff this one! She talks too much.

Enter MYRRHINE.

MYRRHINE

By Phosphoros, the tip of a finger tip
On *her*, and it's two lovely black eyes . . .

MAGISTRATE

What's all this? Officer! *Officer*! Arrest them!
I'm warning you, we can't *have* this sort of thing.

STRATYLLIS *(from the* CHORUS*)*

By Hekate, if he so much as makes a pass at *her*
I'll pull your hairs where it hurts most.
And you can scream your head off.

MAGISTRATE

Not an officer left. But I'll be damned
If I'll be downed by women! Scythians!
Close ranks and prepare to charge!

LYSISTRATA

I'm warning *you*:
We're four companies fully armed and ready.

MAGISTRATE

Up Scythians and at 'em!

LYSISTRATA

Come on, everyone!
All you egg-sellers, greengrocers, garlic-girls,
Bread-sellers, barmaids and all!
Sling 'em, fling 'em, bang 'em, slang 'em!
Do your worst!

A general mêleé. LYSISTRATA*'s speech continues above it.*

Enough! Back there!
Enough! Don't strip the dead.

MAGISTRATE (*gloomily*)
A gory time for my men, and no mistake.

LYSISTRATA
Did you think it was *slaves* you came to fight?
Don't you imagine women thirst for glory?

MAGISTRATE
You *thirst* all right, if there's a bar in sight.

The two CHORUSES *face each other again.*

CHORUS OF MEN (*to* MAGISTRATE)
Hey, you old windbag!
Call yourself one of our rulers?
What's the point of negotiating
With wild beasts?
Don't you know
What sort of a wetting they gave us?

CHORUS OF WOMEN
Was it right to attack
Your neighbours without a reason?
If you do, you must take
Whatever you get – black eyes!
All *I* want to do
Is to sit like a good little virgin,
Meek and mild at home,
Not moving a muscle, *but if you*
Stir up a wasps' nest, be prepared for stings!

CHORUS OF MEN
O Zeus, what shall we do with these dragons?
I can't put up with this! Let's probe
Into this shocking affair:
Why did they want to seize

This Kranaan, inaccessible,
Holy Acropolis up on the rock?

(*To* MAGISTRATE)

Question them, then; take nothing for granted;
Cross-examine them closely;
It'd be culpable negligence not
To get to the bottom of this!

MAGISTRATE
Then first I want to ask: why lock us out of the citadel?

LYSISTRATA
To keep the money safe – so you don't go on fighting for it.

MAGISTRATE
Is money the cause of the war?

LYSISTRATA
Yes, and of every disturbance.
Peisander – anyone – who's ever got into power:
They always stir up trouble, then they can get at the money,
And do what they like with it. Now, not a penny more!

MAGISTRATE
What are you going to do?

LYSISTRATA
Control the Exchequer.

MAGISTRATE
Control the Exchequer, *you*!

LYSISTRATA
Is that so funny?
We do the housekeeping.

MAGISTRATE
That isn't the same.

LYSISTRATA
Why isn't it?

MAGISTRATE
This money's for *war* purposes –

LYSISTRATA
But that's precisely our point: No – more – war.

MAGISTRATE
Then how shall we save the city?

LYSISTRATA
We'll save you!

MAGISTRATE
You?

LYSISTRATA
That's what I said.

MAGISTRATE
Monstrous!

LYSISTRATA
Whether you like it or not.

MAGISTRATE
Ridiculous nonsense!

LYSISTRATA
Why get so cross? That *is* what's going to happen.

MAGISTRATE
Preposterous!

LYSISTRATA
We *must* save you.

MAGISTRATE

Suppose I don't want to be?

LYSISTRATA

All the more reason to.

MAGISTRATE

What's made you dabble
In these matters of peace and war?

LYSISTRATA

If you listen, I'll tell you.

MAGISTRATE

You'd better be brief – or you'll catch it.

LYSISTRATA

Then do *listen* and try to stop clenching your fists.

MAGISTRATE

Dammit, I *can't*! You make me so irritable!

STRATYLLIS (*mocking him*)

You'd *better* try – or you'll catch it!

MAGISTRATE

Be quiet, you old crow!

(*To* LYSISTRATA)

You speak.

LYSISTRATA

Thank you.
All through the war – and what a long war –
By controlling ourselves we managed to endure
Somehow what you men did. We never once
Let ourselves grumble. Not that we approved
What you did do – simply, we understood you.

Oh, how often at home one would hear you spouting
Hot air about something serious! And masking
Our misery with a smile we'd ask you gently,
'Dear, in the Assembly today, did you decide
Anything about peace?' And, 'What's that to do with *you*,'
You'd growl. 'Shut up!' And I did.

STRATYLLIS

I never did!

MAGISTRATE

You'd have been sorry if you hadn't
– Well . . .

LYSISTRATA

I held my tongue. And immediately you'd make
Some even more crazy decision, and I'd sigh and say,
'But how *can* you have passed this lunatic thing?'
And you'd frown and mutter, 'Stick to your spinning,
Or you *will* have something to complain of.
War is men's business.'

MAGISTRATE

And quite right too!

LYSISTRATA

Shouldn't we try to save you from your follies?
When we see you mooning about in the streets moaning
'Isn't there a *man left* in this country?' 'Not one,'
Says the old blimp with you. So we called a rally
Of all the women and planned: *we* would save Greece.
Why wait any longer? Now you must listen to *us* –
It's our turn to talk, and *yours* to be quiet as we've been,
While *we're* busy, putting things right again.

MAGISTRATE

You do that for *us*! Intolerab –

LYSISTRATA

SILENCE!

MAGISTRATE

Told to be quiet by a woman in a veil,
I'd rather die . . .

LYSISTRATA

Oh, if *that's* all it is –
You put my veil on *your* head and be QUIET!

She puts it on him.

KALONIKE
And here's a spindle.

She forces it into his hand.

MYRRHINE

And a *dear* little wool-basket.

LYSISTRATA

Now bundle up your skirt, card wool, and chew beans –
War is women's work!

The MAGISTRATE *is reduced to impotent silence.*

CHORUS OF WOMEN

Come on, women, put down our pitchers and take the field,
We must do our proper bit for the common cause!
Never shall I stop dancing,
Never my knees give,
Nothing I wouldn't dare
For comrades of such metal,
Such spirit and grace and flair,
Such wisdom and love of country,
And such entrancing *sense*!
Born of mettlesome mothers, sharp to molest as nettles,
Let us advance righteous, in anger, and never yield:
The wind stands fair!

LYSISTRATA (*as in prayer*)
But let sweet-spirit Love, let Aphrodite breathe
On our breasts and thighs today
And enflame delight, and quicken
The men to desire, that we
May be called by all the Greeks
Peace-Makers.

MAGISTRATE
Well . . . how will you do it?

LYSISTRATA
First, stop the soldiers
Sloping about the market, like morons, in battle-order.

STRATYLLIS
Indeed we will!

LYSISTRATA
Now, you can see them slopping
Among the stalls, the pots and vegetables, armed to the teeth,
Like Korybantes.

MAGISTRATE
A soldier's a soldier anywhere:
Esprit de corps is essential.

LYSISTRATA
Esprit de corps!
A soldier in full kit, *queueing to buy fish*!

STRATYLLIS
My word, I saw a smart long-haired cavalry captain
Swigging an eggnog from his helmet: bought from an old tart!
Then there was a Thracian so petrified the shop-girl,
Clanking his cutlery, she hopped it, and the dirty
Cheat got his fruit *free* . . .

MAGISTRATE

And how do you propose
To disentangle this and settle everybody?

LYSISTRATA

Easily.

MAGISTRATE

How?

LYSISTRATA

Just as when wool is tangled
We untangle it, working it through
This way and that – so we'll settle the war,
Sending embassies this way and that.

MAGISTRATE

Threads, skeins, spindles, you fool:
What's this to do with *war*?

LYSISTRATA

If you had any sense you could handle
Politics as we do wool!

MAGISTRATE

Well . . . ?

LYSISTRATA

Like the raw fleece in the wash tub, first
You must cleanse the city of dirt:
As *we* beat out the muck and pick out the burrs,
You must pluck out the place-seekers, sack the spongers
Out of their sinecure offices, rip off their heads –
Then the common skein of good sense:
Blend the good aliens, the allies, the strangers,
Even the debtors, into one ball;
Consider the colonies scattered threads,
Pick up their ends and gather them quick;
Make one magnificent bobbin and weave
A garment of government fit for the people!

MAGISTRATE

It's all very well this carding and winding – women!
You haven't any idea what a war *means*.

LYSISTRATA (*very deliberate and serious*)

We know just twice as well.
We bore the sons
You took for soldiers.

MAGISTRATE

Must you recall
Such painful memories?

LYSISTRATA

Yes. And one's young,
And wants to be happy and enjoy one's youth – and all
The men are away. And *we* might bear it – just –
But what about the girls that've never had a man,
Growing old, alone in their beds?

MAGISTRATE

Don't men grow old?

LYSISTRATA

Not like women. When a man comes home
Though he's grey as grief he can always get a girl.
There's no second spring for a woman. None.
She can't recall it, nobody wants her, however
She squanders her time on the promise of oracles,
It's no use . . .

MAGISTRATE (*preening himself*)

Yes, if a man can still stand up for himself . . .

LYSISTRATA (*furious*)

Stand up? Lie down, you dirty old dog!
And it's dead and buried I mean.
Let's get a pig and an urn,
And I'll bake you a sop
For Cerberus – and here's a garland.

She pours water over him.

KALONIKE
And *this* from me.

More water.

MYRRHINE
And this crown from me.

Still more water.

LYSISTRATA
What's the matter? What are you waiting for?
The boat's afloat, and Charon's calling,
You're keeping him from shoving off . . .

MAGISTRATE
This is scandalous! I'm drenched, I've had enough.
I'll go straight to my fellow-officials;
They shall see what a state I'm in!

LYSISTRATA
Are you complaining I haven't laid you out properly?
We'll give you your rites – all in good time! You wait!

The WOMEN *enter the citadel. The* MAGISTRATE *goes off fuming.*

CHORUS OF MEN
No time for sitting about – come on, we're free;
Men, we must strip for action!
Already this seems to me to stink
Of greater trouble and strife – I'm thinking
Of Hippias. There's a whiff of tyranny.
There's no knowing whether
Some Spartan faction
Have put heads together
With Kleisthenes

And inspired these ferocious females with cunning
To seize our money –
The actual cash
That keeps us going!
It's abominable that *women* should boss us citizens
With their babble and cackle of helmets and shields,
And acting on *our* behalf suck up to the Spartans
(Men you can trust – if you trust a ravening wolf).
But what's behind it? A plot to establish a tyranny!
Tyrannize over *me*? Not likely! I'll be on my guard,
I'll keep my sword at the ready, sheathed in myrtle,
And post myself in the market-place beside
The statue of Aristogeiton. And just to begin with –
I'll give this old hag a sock on the jaw!

CHORUS OF WOMEN

Your mother'll hardly know you – you've got so bold!
Girls, we must strip naked!
It's open to anyone to praise
The city – and I, to the end of my days,
Shall love her for giving joy to a gentle child.
I was only seven when I
Carried the Sacred
Vessels; and at ten I
Bore the Temple Mill;
Then in yellow I acted the Little Bear at Brauron,
And, growing taller
And lovelier, took care
Of the Holy Basket – it was heaven!
So don't you think I *want* to give my best to the city?
I was born a woman, yes, but is it my *fault*
If my advice on the present emergency is the sounder?
And I pay my fair share of tax – in the boys I bear.
But you, you wretched old fogeys, what do *you* contribute –
Apart from contriving to squander and waste
Even the Persian Reserve built up by your fathers?
We're running the risk of ruin because of you!
What are you muttering there? You get across *me*,
And I'll take this leather slipper and bash your jaw!

CHORUS OF MEN

This is an outrage! Shall we suffer it? –
And it very much looks to me
As if there's more in the offing!
No man who *is* a man will let this go . . .
Off with our tunics – a man should
Be Man untrammelled from top to toe

Remember how
We comrades stood
For freedom, at Leipsydrion,
When we were young.
And now
We must take wing,
And shake old age off our bodies,
And put youth on!

Give these women an inch, they'll take an ell!
In our manly exercises they'll soon excel!
They'll build ships and sail against us with a fleet!
If they turn to riding, you can write off the knights!
A woman rides well, a gallop won't unseat her!
Look at the Amazons that Mikon depicted fighting
The men, on horseback. No, we've got to check them.
Make pillories and lock them in – *by the neck*!

CHORUS OF WOMEN

By heaven, provoke *me*, I'll make you blubber! –
You'll see my seamy side!
I'll send you yelling to the neighbours!
I'll comb you out, you louse! Now women, up
With your cloaks: a woman should
Be Woman untrammelled from toe to top.

You go for me
In my present mood,
And garlic and beans are off your menu!
Just say the word:
You'll see,

I'll pursue you as hard
As the beetle that got the eagle's
Eggs in the end.

If Lampito loves me and noble Theban Ismenia
You can go to hell, you haven't a hold on me!
Make your decrees sevenfold, you loathsome old fool!
Why, I ask my Boeotian friends for a pretty playmate
For my children on Hecate's day – a sweet little eel –
And 'Sorry we can't; it's against the law', they say.
Your stinking laws – the sort you'll always make,
Till somebody ups with your heels and *breaks your neck*!

*Dance, to mark the passing of time. When it ends, several days have
passed.* LYSISTRATA *comes out of the gateway looking harassed.*

CHORUS OF WOMEN
Lysistrata, why so gloomy? What's the matter?
You, the leader of our glorious . . .

LYSISTRATA
Just the whole nature of women: it makes me despair!

CHORUS OF WOMEN
But *why*?

LYSISTRATA
That's all.

CHORUS OF WOMEN
What ghastly thing has happened?
We're all your friends, you can tell us.

LYSISTRATA
Yes, it *is* ghastly.
I can hardly face telling you, and yet I must.

CHORUS OF WOMEN
Don't bottle it up, my dear. What's the disaster?

LYSISTRATA

The long and short of it is – they're mad for men!

CHORUS OF WOMEN

O Zeus!

LYSISTRATA

No, not Zeus. Men. That's the plain fact. I simply
Can't keep them away from the men another minute.
They just slink out. Why, I caught one chipping away at
The loophole in Pan's Cave; and another wriggling
Down by a block and tackle; another deserting openly;
I dragged one off a sparrow's back by the hair,
Just taking off for Orchilochos' brothel –
They make every sort of excuse to get home. Look!

Enter FIRST WOMAN.

One's coming now. What are *you* doing?

FIRST WOMAN

I just must
Run home for a minute – I left my *best* Milesian
Wool out, and the moths will positively *devour it*.

LYSISTRATA

You and your moths. Inside!

FIRST WOMAN

But I'll come straight back, I *promise*.
I *only* want to spread it out on the couch.

LYSISTRATA

It wouldn't be wool you'd 'only spread'. *No.*

FIRST WOMAN

What, leave it all to be *ruined*?

LYSISTRATA

If necessary, YES.

Enter SECOND WOMAN.

SECOND WOMAN

I'm so *worried* about my flax,
I left it at home unstripped . . .

LYSISTRATA

She's worried about her flax.
Inside! And quick!

SECOND WOMAN

But I *will*
Come back, I swear. I'll just strip it
And come straight back.

LYSISTRATA

No stripping,
Of any sort. You begin and
All the others'll want to, as well.

Enter THIRD WOMAN.

THIRD WOMAN

Oh holy goddess Eileithyia,
Keep my pains in control,
Till I get to some proper place!

LYSISTRATA

What's this?

THIRD WOMAN

My pains have begun!

LYSISTRATA

You weren't pregnant yesterday.

THIRD WOMAN

But I am today. Oh Lysistrata,
I must go home *at once*
To get a midwife . . .

LYSISTRATA

Nonsense!
What's this hard lump you've got?

THIRD WOMAN (*coyly*)

A little boy-baby.

LYSISTRATA

Not this! (*Tapping it.*)
It's hollow and made of brass.
Come off it you fool,
It's the Sacred Helmet! How dare you
Say you were pregnant?

THIRD WOMAN

But I *am*!

LYSISTRATA

Then what's the helmet *for*?

THIRD WOMAN

If my little chick's born here,
In the Acropolis, I'll just pop him
Inside like a dove with its egg.

LYSISTRATA

Excuses and lies! It's perfectly
Clear. You can STAY PUT
Till the naming of your – helmet!

Enter FOURTH WOMAN *and* FIFTH WOMAN.

FOURTH WOMAN

– And I can't sleep a *wink*
Since I saw the Sacred Snake . . .

FIFTH WOMAN
Nor can I. I shall die of *exhaustion*.
Those *wretched* owls – they *never* stop hooting!

LYSISTRATA
You stop lying, you devils! It's your men you want!
Do you think they don't want *us*? What sort of nights
Do you think *they* spend? But you've got to stick to it!
Hold out a little longer, the oracle says
We'll win if we do – just listen to what it says.

WOMEN
The oracle? Tell us! Tell us!

LYSISTRATA
Be quiet, then.

(*In a portentous voice, making it up as she goes.*)

When all the Swallows gather unto One Place, eschewing the
    Hoopoe-birds and their amorous pursuits, then is come the
    end of all Evils, and it is ordained by Zeus the Thunderer
    that the low shall be exalted over the high . . .

STRATYLLIS (*from within*)
Does that mean we lie on top of the men?

LYSISTRATA (*takes no notice*)
But if the Swallows fall into dissensions and fly from the Holy
    Temple, no longer shall they be esteemed virtuous; but
    as wanton and more prone to lechery than all the birds of
    the air!

FIRST WOMAN (*carried away by it all*)
That oracle's plain enough. O all you gods,
Let us not falter now in this extremity of craving.
Let us go back in! We would never live down the disgrace
Of betraying the oracle. Come back inside!

The WOMEN *re-enter the Acropolis. The two* CHORUSES *face each other.*

CHORUS OF MEN

Now
Let me tell you a little story
I heard when I was a boy:
How
There was once a youth called Melanion, who
Was so appalled at the prospect of women he flew
To the mountains rather than marry.
And he hunted hares
And he set his snares,
With his dog there,
And never came home for anyone!
That was the way
He detested women
And we're no less
Wise in our ways than Melanion!

OLD MAN (*in* CHORUS)

Like a smacker, granny?

He makes the sound of a kiss.

OLD WOMAN (*in* CHORUS)

You'll get one you won't like.

OLD MAN

Like a good kick then?

OLD WOMAN

My, what hairs! What a jungle!

OLD MAN

Myronides was black
Bow and stern (ask those who attacked him)
And so was Phormio!

CHORUS OF WOMEN

Now I
will tell you a little story
To offset your Melanion.
Ti-
mon was a man with a beard so prickly
You couldn't get through to his face for the thickets.
He was savage, the son of a Fury.
And, to Timon, men
Were a terrible bane;
He swore like sin,
He vituperated against your vicious nature:
That was the way
He detested you,
And never ceased;
But to women he was the dearest creature.

OLD WOMAN

Like a clip on the jaw?

OLD MAN

Try if you like . . .

OLD WOMAN

Like a good kick then?

OLD MAN

I'd be lost in the jungle . . .

OLD WOMAN

What a lie you're telling!
I may be old, but I still
Can keep myself in trim.

LYSISTRATA *is seen above on the wall.*

LYSISTRATA

Help! Everyone! Quick! This way!

Enter WOMEN *above, with* MYRRHINE.

FIRST WOMAN

What's all the row about?

LYSISTRATA

Look!
A *man*! Have you ever *seen*
A man more obviously
In love? Aphrodite must
Rule him with a rod of iron!

FIRST WOMAN (*prays*)

O Cyprian, Cytherean,
Paphian mistress and guardian,
Keep us to the straight and narrow . . .

(*Eagerly.*)

Where is he? *Who* is he?

LYSISTRATA

Down by Demeter's chapel.

FIRST WOMAN

So he is! Whoever is he?

LYSISTRATA

Does *anyone* know who he is?

MYRRHINE

Yes. My husband, Kinesias.

LYSISTRATA

Then it's your job, Myrrhine,
To lead him up the garden path:
Love him and not love him,
Do *everything* except the
One thing we swore we wouldn't!

MYRRHINE (*with enthusiasm*)

Trust me!

LYSISTRATA (*coolly*)
Of course. *But* I'll stay and help you.
We'll give him the treatment together.
The *rest* of you, go inside.

They all disappear but LYSISTRATA. *Enter* KINESIAS *below,
followed by a* SLAVE *holding a* BABY.

KINESIAS
Oooooh, it's *torture*! I'm racked, I'm wrecked
In a rigid spasm, I'm in agony . . .

LYSISTRATA
Halt! Who goes there!

KINESIAS
I do.

LYSISTRATA
A man?

KINESIAS
Can't you *see* I am?

LYSISTRATA
Then get out!

KINESIAS
And who are you
To throw me out?

LYSISTRATA
The officer
Of the watch.

KINESIAS
Oh heaven,
Do fetch Myrrhine for me . . .

LYSISTRATA

Myrrhine for *you*? Who are *you*?

KINESIAS

Kinesias . . . I'm her husband.

LYSISTRATA

Oh, *Kinesias* . . . we know *you*!
You're famous! Your name's always
On your wife's lips – why, she never
Touches an egg or an apple
But she says 'To Kinesias'.

KINESIAS (*simpers*)

Truly?

LYSISTRATA

Truly . . . and if anyone
Says a word about men, Myrrhine
Immediately swears they're all
Scum but Kinesias!

KINESIAS (*more overpowered*)

Truly?
Oh, *do call her*!

LYSISTRATA

What'll you give me?

KINESIAS

Whatever you like – whatever
I've got. Here – all I can do . . .

Chink of money.

LYSISTRATA

All right. I'll go and *tell* her.

Exit.

KINESIAS

Be quick!
Since she left, the house
Seems horribly empty, I can't
Go in without weeping. I'm utterly
Depressed – I get no kick
Out of food. It's *her* I want.

MYRRHINE (*off*)

Oh yes, of course I love him,
But he won't *let* me love him,
Don't call me out to him . . .

She comes out onto the wall.

KINESIAS

Myrrhine, Myrrhine darling,
What do you mean, not love you?
Come down to me darling . . .

MYRRHINE

No!

KINESIAS

Not when *I* call you, Myrrhine?

MYRRHINE

You *call* – but you don't want me!

KINESIAS

Not want you? I'm dying for you.

MYRRHINE

Good-bye!

She turns to go.

KINESIAS (*wildly*)

But darling, *listen*!
For our child's sake please listen

Aside to the BABY *as he pinches it.*

Here, you little – *call* your mother!

The BABY *yells.*

Haven't you *any* feeling?
Aren't you at all sorry
For our own poor little poppet –

Louder screams.

– Six days unwashed and hungry?

MYRRHINE

I'm very sorry for him.
It's *you* that aren't!

KINESIAS

Then, darling,
Do come down and take him . . .

Still louder screams.

MYRRHINE

What it is to be a mother!
What a life! All right, I'm coming!

She disappears from the wall.

KINESIAS

She looks younger and even sweeter!
When she's aloof and angry
It just makes me want her *more* . . .

MYRRHINE *comes out of the gate and snatches the* BABY.

MYRRHINE

Oh, my angel, my little darling,
Come from your *horrible* daddy,
Come to your mummy, sweetheart . . .

KINESIAS

Why treat me like this, Myrrhine?
We're simply hurting each other.
It's these nasty women have got at you.

MYRRHINE

Don't *touch* me!

KINESIAS

And all our belongings
Going to rack and ruin.

MYRRHINE

Much I care!

KINESIAS

And your knitting
Picked to bits by the hens?

MYRRHINE

I tell you I don't give a damn!

KINESIAS

And the holy rites of marriage
So long neglected? . . . Darling,
Come home.

MYRRHINE

I won't. No . . . unless you,
And all you men, make a treaty
To stop the war.

KINESIAS

If you *want* it,
We'll do it.

MYRRHINE

If you want *me, do it*! –
Then I'll come home. For the present
I've sworn I won't.

KINESIAS

Oh darling,
It's so long I won't . . . Come to me now.

MYRRHINE

No. But that isn't saying
I don't love you . . .

KINESIAS

If you love me,
Why won't you – why . . .

MYRRHINE

You idiot!
Make love in front of the baby?

KINESIAS

Take the boy home, Manes.

Exit SLAVE *with* BABY.

There! He's gone. *Now* won't you?

MYRRHINE

But where can we *go*, darling?

KINESIAS

Pan's cave. Couldn't be better.

MYRRHINE

But there's my purification,
Before going back to the citadel . . .

KINESIAS
Easy. The spring of Klepsydra.

MYRRHINE
But I've sworn an oath; do you want me
To break it?

KINESIAS
I'll take the consequences.
Put *that* out of your head.

MYRRHINE
But we need a bed. I'll get one . . .

KINESIAS
We can lie on the ground, can't we?

MYRRHINE
You on the dirty ground?
Darling, I'd *never* let you.

Exit inside.

KINESIAS *(to himself)*
She loves me, oh *how* she loves me!
It's as plain as my pikestaff!

Re-enter MYRRHINE *with bed.*

MYRRHINE
Now hurry up and lie down.
I'll take off my things – *oh dear*,
I must go and get a mattress!

KINESIAS
But I don't want a mattress!

MYRRHINE
Oh, but you do, it's beastly
On the bare cords.

KINESIAS

Give me a kiss then?

MYRRHINE (*slaps him*)

There!

Exit inside.

KINESIAS

Ow! Do come back quickly!

Re-enter MYRRHINE *with mattress.*

MYRRHINE

Here's the mattress. Lie down.
I'll take off my things – *oh dear,*
I must go and get a pillow!

KINESIAS

But I don't want a pillow!

MYRRHINE

But I do!

Exit inside.

KINESIAS

I'm simply starving:
I'm being kept waiting longer
Than Heracles for his dinner.

Re-enter MYRRHINE *with pillow.*

MYRRHINE

Lift up your head, darling.

KINESIAS

I've got everything . . .

MYRRHINE (*slowly*)
I wonder,
Have we got all we want?

KINESIAS
All but you. Quick, my treasure!

MYRRHINE
I'm undoing my girdle, but remember –
No cheating over the treaty!

KINESIAS
I'd rather die.

MYRRHINE
But darling,
You haven't got any blankets!

KINESIAS
I don't *want* any blankets,
I just want *you*!

MYRRHINE
In a minute;
I'll be as quick as I can . . .

Exit inside.

KINESIAS
She's killing me with her blankets.

Re-enter MYRRHINE *with blankets.*

MYRRHINE
Up a moment!

KINESIAS
I'm up, all right.

MYRRHINE
Would you like a dash of perfume?

KINESIAS
No, by Apollo, I wouldn't.

MYRRHINE
By Aphrodite you would,
Whether you like it or not.

Exit inside.

KINESIAS
Oh Zeus, make her spill the bottle!

Re-enter MYRRHINE *with scent bottle.*

MYRRHINE
Put out your hand, take it
And rub it in.

KINESIAS
By Apollo!
It stinks – of delay, not love!

MYRRHINE
Oh! I've brought you the wrong bottle.
This is the cheapest Rhodian . . .

KINESIAS
All *right*, it'll do.

MYRRHINE
Nonsense!

Exit inside.

KINESIAS
Damn the man who invented scent!

Re-enter MYRRHINE *with new scent.*

MYRRHINE

Just hold this bottle will you?

KINESIAS

For god's sake don't go getting
Anything else – lie down,
And see what I've got for you . . .

MYRRHINE

I will, darling, I will.
There go my shoes, and Kinesias –
You *will* vote for peace, won't you?

She runs through the gate. It clangs shut behind her.

KINESIAS

Oh, *that*, yes, I'll . . . God in heaven, she's gone!
She's tricked me! She's left me standing!
I've been robbed of the loveliest girl in the world! –
But I must have *someone*!
Or how will you ever grow up,
My poor little hungry orphan?
Where's Kynalopex? Quick –
Send me a nurse, from your brothel!

CHORUS OF MEN

Poor old cock! You're in a terrible way!
What distress of soul – I'm really sorry for you!
These pangs of unemployment
Are more than a body can bear . . .

KINESIAS

O Zeus, what misery!

CHORUS OF MEN

And *she* did this to you!
The utterly foul, entirely repulsive –

KINESIAS

– Darling. No, she's *sweet*, utterly *sweet*!

CHORUS OF MEN

Sweet is she?
Sweet as muck! O Zeus, Zeus, suck
Her up in a whirlwind, spin
Her round like a ball, then let her fall
From a very great height
Right on the tip of my family tree!

The CHORUS *fall back. Enter from one side* MAGISTRATE, *from the other a* SPARTAN HERALD.

HERALD

Hey! Can you tell me the way
To the Senate? I've got some news.

MAGISTRATE

News? And who may *you* be?
A man, or Priapos in person?

HERALD

A herald from Sparta, mate,
With news of a treaty.

MAGISTRATE

A treaty?
With a spear under your cloak?

HERALD (*slowly*)

No . . .
I haven't a spear . . .

MAGISTRATE

Why turn
Away? Why fiddle with your cloak then?
Are you stiff from your journey?

HERALD

The man's nuts!

MAGISTRATE

But *look* at you.

HERALD

It's no joke!

MAGISTRATE

Then what is it?

HERALD

A Spartan secret dispatch.

MAGISTRATE

If *that's* a secret dispatch,
I've got one, too.
Come on, tell me the truth:
How are things in Sparta?
I know the situation.

HERALD

Grim. It's all up with us.
And all our allies.

MAGISTRATE

How did the trouble begin? Was it Pan?

HERALD

No, it was Lampito,
Then all the blasted women,
Kicked us out of bed.

MAGISTRATE

And how do you like *that*?

HERALD

It's no fun at all. We creep
About the town, bent double

Like we were carrying lanterns
In a gale. And the women won't
Let us so much as tickle
Their fancies till we make
Peace for the whole of Greece.

MAGISTRATE

I see the whole thing: it's a nation-
Wide plot by the women. Go quickly
And get your authorities
To send envoys with absolute powers
To make peace. I'll persuade our Council.
I can put it to them straight.

HERALD

That's proper talk, mate. I'm off home.

Exeunt.

CHORUS OF MEN

Women! There is nothing worse – not fire nor a leopard!

CHORUS OF WOMEN

Then why attack us when you might have had us as an ally?

CHORUS OF MEN

Women! Could one *ever* cease one's hatred?

CHORUS OF WOMEN

As you like it,
But seeing you all naked I don't like it – you're a figure
Of fun! Come here to me and let me put you on your tunic!

CHORUS OF MEN

Kind of you . . . I must admit I stripped it off in anger.

CHORUS OF WOMEN

Now look a man and not a joke! *If* you'd not annoyed me
I'd have taken out the fly that's milling in your eye now.

CHORUS OF MEN

So *that's* what has been aggravating me – the damn mosquito:
Scoop it out and show it me – it's been at me for ages.

CHORUS OF WOMEN

I will. But *why* must you behave so tetchily? Good heavens!
What a monster! Do you see? From the Trikorysian marshes!

CHORUS OF MEN

Bored clean through my head it has, and though you've got it
     out, my
Tears keep flowing . . .

CHORUS OF WOMEN

I'll wipe your eyes, although you've been so brutal,
And I'll love you . . .

CHORUS OF MEN

No, you won't.

CHORUS OF WOMEN

Say what you like, *I'll love you*!

CHORUS OF MEN

Get on with you, you flatterers! Was there ever a truer saying:
'Impossible to live with you. Impossible without you.'
But now I'll make a treaty, from henceforth for everlasting,
I'll never raise a finger against you, *and* VICE VERSA! –
Let's start the ball rolling. *You* strike up an anthem.

CHORUS OF WOMEN

Men! We're not prepared to
Slander anybody, but,
Quite to the con-trary,
Say and do the kindest things:
There's misery enough.
So let it be announced to
Any man or woman who
Wants a bit of money –
They can borrow it, our purses

Are simply *stuffed* (with nothing),
And if the peace is ratified,
And everybody gratified,
They needn't pay us back.

We've organised a dinner
For some playboys from Carystos
(Such *manners*) – minestrone
Is in the pot and suckling pig's
The *plat du soir*.
It's luscious and delicious,
So have an early bath and come,
And bring *all* your children –
Just walk in as if it were
Your own front door! –
I'm *sure* you'll never grudge it if
You find you cannot budge it, if
It's bolted in your face!

Enter the SPARTAN AMBASSADORS.

CHORUS OF MEN

Look at the ambassadors from Sparta!
Are they on crutches? They're stooping along, their beards
Almost trailing to the ground. Greetings, you Spartans!
How are you?

SPARTAN AMBASSADOR

You can see. Do we need to answer?

CHORUS OF MEN

This disaster keeps on mounting.

SPARTAN AMBASSADOR

True enough.
But what can a man say? We simply *must*
Have peace, however we get it.

CHORUS OF MEN

And here come our delegates:
– Whatever's the matter?
Have you got athlete's arm?

Enter the ATHENIAN AMBASSADOR.

ATHENIAN AMBASSADOR

Can *anyone* say
Where Lysistrata is? You can see
What terrible shape we're in.

CHORUS OF MEN

We're all the same.
When d'you find it worst? When you first wake?

ATHENIAN AMBASSADOR

It gets me up as much as it gets me down!
If we don't make peace pretty soon, heaven help us,
We'll have to fall back on Kleisthenes!

CHORUS OF MEN

Take my advice
And put your clothes on.
Don't you remember how they mutilated the Hermai?

ATHENIAN AMBASSADOR

Heavens yes! Thank you.

SPARTAN AMBASSADOR *(aside)*

Right enough. I'll put on mine.

ATHENIAN AMBASSADOR *(approaching)*

Gretings, Spartans! This is a bad business.

SPARTAN AMBASSADOR

It is, that!

(*Aside*)

Lucky they didn't see us
A minute ago, we might have pricked their vanity.

ATHENIAN AMBASSADOR
Let's get down to it at once. Why've you come?

SPARTAN AMBASSADOR
To discuss peace.

ATHENIAN AMBASSADOR
Excellent! So have we.
Shall we send for Lysistrata? She's the only one
Can bring us to terms.

SPARTAN AMBASSADOR
Get Lysis-whoever-you-like
Who can settle t'matter.

ATHENIAN AMBASSADOR
No need for us to call.
She must have heard us talking and here she is.

LYSISTRATA *comes out attended by a very pretty girl,*
RECONCILIATION.

CHORUS OF MEN
Lysistrata! Incomparable woman!
Now is your hour of greatness! You must
– Be uncompromising,
– Be clement,
– Be stern,
– Be conciliatory,
– Be wayward,
– Be wise,
For you hold the leading statesmen of this land
In the palm of your beautiful hand: and we entrust you
With our common fate!

It is for you to settle, for ever and finally,
All dispute!

LYSISTRATA

Not such a difficult matter (unless you take
To taking each other to bed and I shall soon
Know if you do!)
Where's Reconciliation?

RECONCILIATION *comes forward.*

Now, my dear, go and fetch those Spartans. Don't tug them
In the boorish way our husbands do with us;
Be thoroughly feminine – but if they *won't*
Give you their hands, take them and tow them, *politely*,
By their . . . life-lines. Then fetch the Athenians too,
And if they won't take your hand, grab hold of whatever they
    offer . . .

The AMBASSADORS *are brought to her.*

Now, you Spartans: Stand near me, *here* please.
And you Athenians, *there* – and listen to me.
I may be only a woman, but I've got sense.
Partly I was born with it (and plenty of it),
Partly I listened to my father, my elders and betters –
I wasn't so ill-taught.
So first I propose
To censure you both equally (and perfectly rightly),
You! Who have hallowed altars from one and the same ewer,
Like blood relations at Olympia –
Thermopylai – Delphi – and many another place
Will spring to your minds – and yet, I say, and YET,
With a barbarian army mobilized
And ready to pounce, you have engrossed yourselves
In the destruction of your cities –
In the death of your own people!

ATHENIAN AMBASSADOR

I'm dying for you, darling!

LYSISTRATA

Listen! Spartans, I turn to you: Perikleidas!
Does that name mean *nothing* to you?
Have you forgotten how he came here, knelt at our altars,
Pale in his purple robe, and begged for help? –
You were hard-pressed by Messene; there was an earthquake
And Kimon came to your help with a force four thousand strong
And saved all Sparta! –
And, even so, you ravage
The land of your friends!

ATHENIAN AMBASSADOR

They're wrong, Lysistrata!

SPARTAN AMBASSADOR

We're wrong, admitted we're wrong.
But what a ravishing
Bottom she's got . . .

LYSISTRATA

Do you think I've nothing to say to you Athenians?
You – in the livery of slaves – have you forgotten
How the Spartans came and slaughtered those Thessalians,
And how many others of Hippias' gang?
Who else was your friend that day? Who else
Restored you the cloak of freedom? Oh, don't you see?

SPARTAN AMBASSADOR

I've never seen a more desirable woman.

ATHENIAN AMBASSADOR

I've never seen more clearly what I want!

LYSISTRATA

Bound by such mutual ties, how *can* you bear
To fight each other and bicker and squabble and scrap
And never cease? Make peace! Make peace! Why not?

SPARTAN AMBASSADOR
Give us back our breast-work and we're ready –

ATHENIAN AMBASSADOR
Your – *what?*

SPARTAN AMBASSADOR
Pylos. It's never out of our thoughts.

ATHENIAN AMBASSADOR
By god, no!

LYSISTRATA
Go on, give it them, why not?

ATHENIAN AMBASSADOR
What trouble spot'd we have?

LYSISTRATA
Ask for something *else* in exchange –

The ATHENIAN AMBASSADOR *illusrates his points on*
RECONCILIATION, *as if she were a map.*

That's tricky. Well, suppose they give us Echinos there,
With its delta, and the Melian gulf behind and all
That's enclosed by the legs of Megara . . .

SPARTAN AMBASSADOR
You're mad!
You can't have everything!

LYSISTRATA
Don't argue about the legs!

ATHENIAN AMBASSADOR
I'd like to strip and plough my bit of land.

SPARTAN AMBASSADOR

I'd like to fertilise mine, I'm telling you.

LYSISTRATA

Then come to terms and you'll be able to!
If you *really* want to, go and discuss the matter
With your allies.

ATHENIAN AMBASSADOR

Why waste time? Our allies
Stand exactly where we do, all they want
Is what we want – our women!

SPARTAN AMBASSADOR

That goes for ours –

ATHENIAN AMBASSADOR

And certainly the Karystians.

LYSISTRATA

Very well, then! Go and purify yourselves
And we'll give you a banquet here
In the Acropolis tonight
On what we can rake together.
We'll make our treaty then,
And each of you can take
His wife and go home again.

ATHENIAN AMBASSADOR

My dear, we'll go at once.

SPARTAN AMBASSADOR

Show me the way, brother.

ATHENIAN AMBASSADOR

Quicker than light.

Exeunt.

CHORUS OF WOMEN

Just *anything* in my wardrobe –
The run of my jewel-case –
(I'm just that sort of person),
It's all on loan, you can choose
For your daughter the Basket-Bearer
Elect, or for *any* child!
It's all there for the taking,
Nothing is so well sealed
That you can't break in a sample
Whatever's inside – it's free!
But if you set eyes on the tiniest speck
You've sharper eyes than me.
Are any of you starving
With servants to support?
Or a horde of hungry children?
I've a house full of fine wheat,
And loaves for a whole day's ration!
If any of the poor
Will bring their sacks and baskets,
No one can stuff in more
Than my nice young fellow, Manes . . .
But kindly get this right:
If you come too close to my door,
Beware of the dog. He'll bite!

It is now evening. There is a PORTER *on the gate. The feast is going*
on   inside. Two ATHENIAN YOUTHS *hammer on the door.*

FIRST YOUTH

Oi! Be a sport, and let us in!

PORTER

Clear off, you!

FIRST YOUTH

Come on do! Shall I tickle your arse
With a torch? No! That'd be *vulgar*!
I'd never do *that* – but if the audience'd *like* it . . .
Would you?

SECOND YOUTH

'Ere, I'll 'elp.

PORTER

Hop it, you two!
Or I'll pull your hair off. Git aht of it
So these Spartans inside can go 'ome
In peace – when they've done drinking.

> *Two* ATHENIAN BANQUET GUESTS *come out.*
> *They are rather drunk.*

FIRST GUEST

Well, I never saw such a spread!
Folly good Jellows these Spartans –
Never known you in better form,
Ol' boy, what wit, what? – 's the WINE.

SECOND GUEST

'S it. When we're sober, we're mad.
Now, I'll give the Gov'ment a tip –
Always keep our Ambassadors tight!
Right! Why? – Go to Sparta sober,
'Mediately look for trouble.
Don't listen to a word they say
Or what they don't say – see?
Then all come back with conflic –
Conflickering reports. 'Sno good.
Now, everything's all right.
If they sing 'The Minstrel Boy' –

> *Does so.*

When they ought to sing 'Come Landlord fill the flowing bowl' –

> *Does so.*

Clap 'em on the back, praise 'em,
Swear they were right . . .

Laughter from YOUTHS.

PORTER

Blast you two kids, git aht of it, will yer!

FIRST YOUTH (*going*)

Not 'alf. The high-ups are comin' – they're high, all right!

Exeunt YOUTHS. *Enter* SPARTAN *and* ATHENIAN
AMBASSADORS, *with* MUSICIANS. *They, too, have all
had too much to drink.*

SPARTAN AMBASSADOR (*careful of his words*)

Here, lad, take the pipes
And we'll do a song and dance
In honour of the Athenians –
And ourselves, come to that.

ATHENIAN AMBASSADOR

Yes, take the pipes, boy. We'd be delighted.

SPARTANS (*as* CHORUS)

Memory, awaken
The Muse of your youth! Sing
How we and the Athenians
Put paid to the bloody Persians
At Artemision –
And pounded their fleet to pulp!
Ah, we were gods then.

Leonidas was our leader
And we whetted our tusks like boars
And the sweat from our jaws ran slavering,
We were blood to the knees – the Persians
Outnumbered us ten to one.
But not by the end of the day!
Ah, we were gods then.

O woodland Artemis,
Huntress, virgin goddess,
Hither descend and bless
Our treaty:
And by thy divine grace
May our friendship flourish
And year by year increase,
Without deceit.
O virgin huntress
Descend and bless!

Enter LYSISTRATA.

LYSISTRATA (*gently*)

Now all is well; all is well.
O Spartans, O Athenians, take
Your wives. Let every man
With his beloved dance for joy
And bless the gods for this event –
And may we never never make
Wars in the world again.

ATHENIANS (*as* CHORUS))

Dance then, oh dance for joy!
Gather the Graces
And Artemis and her heavenly
Brother Apollo; bid
Bacchus, his eyes blazing
In a maze of Maenads; summon
Zeus in his robe of thunder,
His Queen serene beside him;
Call the Holy Witnesses
To celebrate this peace!
The peace that Aphrodite
The darling goddess made!
Alalai! *Lalai*!
Lift up your voices – sing
For victory, for peace!
Let all your voices ring

For victory, for peace!
Evoi! Evoi! Evoi!

ATHENIAN VOICE

Spartans, *you* sing a *new* song,
Another song, for us!

SPARTANS (*as* CHORUS)

Come down, O Muse, from Taygetos, and praise Apollo of
     Amyclai,
And the Queen of the brazen Temple
And Castor and Pollux at play
On the banks of Eurotas – O!
But the dance, the dance, the dance!
Honour the city of Sparta
That loves the divine dance!
– Whose girls on the banks of Eurotas
Fleet-foot as fillies prance,
And flounce their flying hair
Like Bacchanals as they bear
Their emblems on, and there
The holy, the comely daughter
Of the Swan leads the dance!

O follow, O bind your hair,
Leap like a deer and sing
Anthem in unison:
Cheer the All-Conquering,
The Goddess, the All-Powerful,
     ATHENE! ATHENE!
     ATHENE! ATHENE!

End of the play.

Glossary

Acharnai – (a-KAR-ni). Mining village near Athens

Acropolis – (a-KROP-o-liss, 'high city'). Rocky outcrop in the centre of Athens, with a fortified castle at the top including the Parthenon (temple of Athene)

Adonis – (a-DOH-niss). In myth, a hunky mortal loved by Aphrodite, who died. Sobbing his name and sighing was said (in comedy) to be a favourite activity of women

Alalai! *Lalai*! – (a-la-la-EE, la-la-EE). Ecstatic cries sung at festivals of the gods – thought to be part of the language of the gods. See also *Evoi*!

Amazons – warrior-women from the far North. In myth, King Theseus of Athens married their queen Antiope and then deserted her. The Amazons attacked Athens, and were defeated. This battle was one of those proudly carved on the marble facades of the Parthenon

Amyklai – (am-IK-lie). Town in the Peloponnese, said in myth to be the birthplace of Castor and Pollux

Anagyros – (an-A-gi-ross). Swampy area near Athens, famous for its stink

Aphrodite – (aff-ro-DIE-tee). Goddess of beauty and sex

Apollo – (a-POL-loh). God of the Sun and of prophecy, particularly worshipped by men

Artemis – (AR-te-miss). Goddess of childbirth and protector of women

Artemision – (ar-tem-i-SEE-on). Coastal area where the Greek fleet defeated the Persians sixty years before *Lysistrata*

Athene – (ath-EE-nee). Goddess of war and wisdom, patron of Athens

Aristogeiton – (a-rist-o-GAY-tohn). (Real) revolutionary, who freed Athens from tyranny a century before *Lysistrata*. One of the city's great popular heroes

Bacchic – 'of Bacchus' ('Bacchus' was the name given to Dionysos, god of wine, by his followers during their orgies)

beetle that got the eagle's eggs – in one of Aesop's fables, an eagle built its nest higher and higher to prevent the eggs being stolen, but a determined beetle climbed and climbed until it reached them

Boeotia – (bee-OH-sha). Farming area in central Greece, famous in comedy for yokels. Neutral during the Peloponnesian War

Boupalos – (BOO-pa-loss). (Real) boxer, famous for his huge punches

Brauron – (BRAV-ron). Village near Athens, where there was a temple of Artemis. Aristocratic girls took part in solemn puberty-rituals there, first dancing in bear-costumes, then, two or three years later, carrying the basket and corn grains sacred to the goddess. These ceremonies marked their official entry to adulthood

Castor and Pollux – in myth, twin sons of Zeus and the mortal

queen Leda of Sparta. 'Castor and Pollux!' was a favourite Spartan oath

Charon – (KA-rohn). In myth, the boatman who ferried dead souls to the Underworld

Clepsydra – (kleps-ID-ra). In myth, a nymph chased by Pan, and turned by the gods into a water-spring, in the nick of time

Corybantes – (kor-i-BANT-es, 'crested ones'). In myth, whirling dancers

Cyprian – (SIP-ri-an). 'the Cyprian' (that is, 'the one from Cyprus') was a name for Aphrodite, said in myth to have been born there

Cytherean – (sith-EE-ree-an). Honorary name of Aphrodite, who was said first to have come to Earth there

Delphi – (DEL-fee). Apollo's prophetic shrine on Mount Parnassos. All visitors had to swear an oath of peace

Demeter – (de-MEE-ter). Goddess of harvest, particularly worshipped by women

Demostratos – (dem-o-STRAH-toss, 'people's army'). (Real) politician, a fiery war-speaker

Drakes – (DRAH-kees, 'eagle-eyes'). Old Athenian in the Chorus

Echinos – (e-KEE-noss). A real place, but used here because it meant 'vagina' in slang

Eileithyia – (i-lith-EE-a). Goddess of the pains of childbirth

Euripides – (yoo-RIP-i-dees, Greek yoo-ri-PEE-dees). Athenian playwright often mocked by Aristophanes (who may have been his friend)

Eurotas – (you-ROH-tass). River of Sparta

Evoi! – (e-voh-EE). Ecstatic cry sung in honour of Dionysos: supposed to represent the language of the gods themselves. See also *Lalai! Lalai!*

Hekate – (hek-AH-tee). Goddess of black magic

Helen – ('Moonlike'). Queen of Sparta in myth, the most beautiful woman in the world. Prince Paris of Troy stole her, so starting the Trojan War

Herakles – (HER-a-klees, Greek he-ra-KLEES, 'glory of Hera'). In myth, hero-son of Zeus, famed both for fighting monsters and for gluttony. 'By Herakles' was a favourite oath with old soldiers

Hermai – (HERM-eye). Statues of Hermes, placed outside people's houses. They had erect penises, which you stroked for good luck as you went in or out. In a drunken escapade one night, the playboy general Alcibiades and his friends chopped the penises off all the Hermai – a scandal

Hippias – (hip-PEE-ass). (Real) political agitator and tyrant of a century earlier

Ismenia – (is-men-EE-a). Name given to Theban women, after the Theban river Ismenos

Kalonike – (kal-on-EE-kee, 'fine victory'). Lysistrata's neighbour

Karystos – (kar-ISS-toss). Karystos was an Athenian ally during the Peloponnesian War, but comedians claimed that it was because Karystian women were hideous, and Karystian men wanted Athenians instead

Kerberos – (KER-ber-oss, 'pit devil'). In myth, the three-headed guard-dog of the Underworld. To get past him you offered him a 'sop' – a piece of meat, drugged

LYSISTRATA

Kimon – (KI-mohn). (Real) Athenian general who helped the Spartans defeat the Messenians

Kinesias – (kin-e-SEE-ass, 'randy'). Myrrhine's husband

Kleisthenes – (klis-THAY-nees). (Real) Athenian, regularly mocked by Aristophanes because he liked to dress as a woman and was a coward in battle

Kleomenes – (klee-o-MAY-nees). (Real) Spartan king of the past, who invaded Athens, was trapped in the Acropolis and starved into surrender

Kolias (ko-LEE-ass). Short for 'Aphrodite of Kolias'. Aphrodite had a temple in the seaside village of Kolias, and (in comedy) it was claimed that sex-orgies happened there

Kranaan – (kran-AH-an, 'rocky'). Name for the Acropolis

Kynalopex – (kin-a-LOH-peks). Brothel-keeper, real or imaginary

Laches – (LA-kees, 'miner'). Old Athenian from the Chorus

Lampito – (lam-pi-TOH, 'her Excellency'). Spartan woman

Leipsydrion – (leep-si-DREE-on). Site of a battle during the war which ended Hippias' tyranny

Lemnos – (LEM-noss). Greek island, famous in Aristophanes' time for 'Lemnos fire', pitch-soaked cloth tied to arrows and lit just before they were shot

Leonidas – (le-on-EE-dass). Real Spartan leader against the Persians

Lykon – (LIK-ohn, 'wolf-like'). Old Athenian in the Chorus

Lysistrata – (liss-i-STRAH-ta, 'looser of armies'). Athenian woman

Maenads – (MEE-nads, 'wild ones'). Orgiastic dancers who worshipped Dionysos

Manes – (MAH-nees). Slave

Marathon – (MA-ra-thohn). Coastal village near Athens, where the Greeks defeated a huge Persian army in the Persian Wars seventy years before *Lysistrata*

Melanion – (mel-an-EE-on). In myth, a misogynist who nevertheless successfully ran a race with Atalanta, the fastest runner on Earth, who had promised sex to any man who beat her

Menelaus – (men-e-LAY-oss, 'leader'). Spartan king in the myth-story of the Trojan War; married to Helen, the most beautiful woman in the world